MIND YOUR LANGUAGE
2

Sue Palmer
and
Peter Brinton

Oliver & Boyd

Illustrations by Scoular Anderson and Trevor Carter
Cover illustration by Trevor Carter

To Matthew and Beth

Oliver & Boyd
Longman House
Burnt Mill
Harlow
Essex CM20 2JE

An Imprint of Longman Group UK Ltd

ISBN 0 05 004050 2
First published 1988
Fifth impression 1992

Set in Linotron Aster 14 on 16 pt

Printed in Hong Kong
SWT/05

Contents

What is Language For?

This book is called *Mind Your Language*. It will help you to think about the language you speak and write. We all use language every day.

We use language in lots of different ways. In the pictures, the boy is using language in these ways:

1) to say what he wants
2) to entertain somebody
3) to ask a question
4) to help sort out his thoughts
5) to warn people.

Which picture is which?

How is language being used in the next four pictures?

Working without language

Life would be very difficult without language. How might you show people what you mean, if you could not use language?

Work in groups of about 4 or 5. You are going to make up a little play, based on a well-known fairy story or nursery rhyme. But it must be a play *without language*. And you must practise it *without language*.

1) You have a few minutes in your group to decide which fairy story or nursery rhyme to act out. You may talk about this. *Keep it secret from the rest of the class.*
2) You have about five minutes to practise your play. But you may not talk. Language is banned!
3) Your teacher will choose a few groups to act out their plays. Remember – no words are allowed.
   The rest of the class can try to guess what story or rhyme it is. (If nobody can guess, your teacher might let you try it again, using words this time.)

Would it be easy to live without language?
How long do you think your class could manage to get on without language? Perhaps sometime your teacher will let you try a Class Silence, and see how long you can keep it up!

So far we have thought about *spoken language*.
But we can also write language down. In the next
picture there are lots of examples of *written language*.
How many different examples of writing can you see?
What are they?

Written language is used in many ways too. The
examples of writing in this picture use language for
many different purposes. What is the purpose of the
written language in each example – *what is it for*?

What problems would these people have if there was
no such thing as writing?

doctors   shoppers
  story-tellers
postmen   cooks
          YOU
  teachers   travellers

Working without written language

Before writing was invented, some people used picture-writing instead. Here is an example of the sort of way pictures can be used to send a message.

What do you think it means? What are the problems in working out the meaning?
(The message the "writer" intended is on page 18.)

Try some picture-writing for yourself on scrap paper. Think of something that someone might want to write down – a story, a message, a letter, even a shopping list. Try to show it in very *simple* pictures.

When you have finished, see if other people in the class can make sense of your picture-writing.

Perhaps the best examples can be drawn again neatly, to be displayed on the wall.

Common and Proper Nouns

<u>Sarah</u> and <u>Marie</u> gave the <u>book</u> to their <u>teacher</u>.

All the words underlined in the sentence above are *nouns*. What are nouns?

Which words are nouns in the following sentences?

The baker sold bread, cakes and biscuits.
Frankenstein made a monster in his laboratory.

A noun is the name of a person, place or thing.

ABCDEFGHIJKLM
abcdefghijklm

Alphabetical Shopkeepers

My name is Alice;
My husband's name is
 Archibald;
We live in America,
And we sell apples.

My name is Basil;
My wife's name is
 Barbara;
We live in Barcelona,
And we sell bicycles.

My name is Clara;
My husband's name is
 Clarence;
We live in a cupboard
And we sell cheese.

Take it in turns round the class to invent alphabetical
shopkeepers like the ones above. (You may have to
miss out X, Y and Z!) All the names of people, places
and things that you make up will be *nouns*.

10

Some of the nouns in the alphabetical shopkeepers game begin with a capital letter when they are written down. They are called **proper nouns**. Some begin with a small letter. They are called **common nouns**.

Look at the common and proper nouns in the speech bubbles on page 10. What is special about proper nouns that makes us give them a capital letter when we write them down?

Why don't common nouns get a capital letter?

Note: some proper nouns are made up of two or more words. All parts of the names begin with capital letters.

Mr. Brown

River Thames

Atlantic Ocean

Royal Opera House

John Smith

Black Beauty

Manchester United

High Street

Little Red Riding Hood   Prince William Dr. Who Bugs Bunny   Mount Evere

August   Thursday   Black Beauty   Birmingham   River Thames

Above are some proper nouns. For each of them, think of a common noun which tells you what it is. Your teacher can write them up on the board like this:

Proper noun	Common noun that tells you what it is
Cinderella	girl

or you could write woman or orphan or maid

At the foot of the page are some common nouns. For each one, think of a proper noun that is the special name for one particular example. Your teacher can write them up on the board like this:

or you could write Cardiff or London or Glasgow or Belfast

Common noun	Proper noun that is the special name for one example
city	Manchester

school   boy town   mountain   street   teacher

girl   month   pop-star   man

dog   cat   gold-fish   footballer   day

Do you usually put the little word "a" in front of most proper nouns? (for example, "a Dr. Who")
Do you put it in front of common nouns? (for example, "a man")
Why do you think this is?

There are plenty of proper nouns to do with *your* life – your own name, the name of the road and town that you live in, your school's name, the name of the month you were born.
Go round the class and quickly give:

1) your forename
2) your surname
3) the name of the month you were born
4) the names of any pets you have.

In your language book:

Write the heading – *Common and Proper Nouns*

A Copy and complete this passage. Look back to the chapter if you are not sure about what words are missing from the spaces.

A n_____ is the name of a p_____, p_____ or th_____.

   C_____ nouns refer to p_____, p_____s and th_____s in general. They begin with small letters.

   P_____ nouns are special names for particular examples of p_____, p_____s and t_____s. They begin with c_____ letters.

B Copy out this form and fill it in for yourself:

A Form About Me

My forename: _____

My surname: _____

My address: _____

_____

My school: _____

My birth month: _____

My pets' names (if none, write "None"): _____

My favourite day of the week: _____

C Draw two columns in your book and label them like this: –

Proper Nouns	common nouns
1 Dr. Who	man
2 Black Beauty	horse
3 Mount Everest	
4 Cinderella	
5 Birmingham	
6 Bugs Bunny	
7 August	
8	
9	
10	

In the Proper Noun column, copy 10 of the proper nouns you can find on page 12. We have started you off to show what we mean.

In the other column, put one common noun which goes with each of the proper nouns. The first two are done for you.

Draw two columns in your book and label them like this:

Proper Nouns	common nouns
Sally	1 girl
Snowdon	2 mountain
	3 dog
	4 pop-star
	5 day
	6 cat
	7
	8
	9
	10

In the common noun column, list 10 of the common nouns you can find on page 12. We have started you off to show what we mean.

In the other column, put one proper noun to go with each of the common nouns. The first two are done for you to show what we mean.

Have all your Proper Nouns got Capital Letters at the beginning?
Have all your common nouns got small letters?

D Copy out these sentences. Put a ring round every common noun. Underline every proper noun.

1) Sarah and Marie gave the book to their teacher.
2) The baker sold bread, cakes and biscuits.
3) Frankenstein made a monster in his laboratory.

E Copy out these sentences, putting capital letters at the beginning of all proper nouns.

1) mr. jenkins always goes to france for his holidays.
2) The name of francis drake's ship was the golden hind.
3) black beauty is a book by anna sewell.
4) celtic and rangers are football teams in glasgow.

Note! Book titles are proper nouns too! They get capital letters.

School Dinners by Terry Bull

Waterproof Clothing by Anna Rack

The First Noel by Carol Singer

Join the Army by Stan Dubstraight

Gardening by Dan D. Lion

How to Scrub Floors by Neil Ingdown

My Life of Crime by Robin Banks

The Joy of Slimming by Anita Figure

3 Verbs and Sentences

Have you ever tried *scrudging*?

When you feel you need to scrudge, you screw your face up, put your arms round your head, pull your knees up as far as you can under your chin, and try to make yourself disappear. It is sometimes helpful to scrudge when you feel fed up. Try it now.

If anyone has managed to disappear, you'd better report it to the headteacher. If not, look at these words:

galumphing   **blooging**   **pittering**

How would you galumph? Or pitter? Or bloog?
Your teacher will choose some people to show you for each word.

Scrudge, galumph, pitter and bloog are all made-up words of **doing** or **being**. Words of doing or being are called *verbs*.

Think of some real verbs, and put your hand up to tell the teacher.

A verb is a word of *doing* or *being*.

Every *sentence* must have a verb. A group of words which does not have a verb is not a sentence. It is called a *phrase*. Which of these are sentences and which are phrases?

Come over here!

Sir Edmund Hillary climbed Everest in 1953.

The car skidded to a halt.

London, capital city of England

Sit down!

The big black cat

Can cheetahs run faster than any other animal?

No!

What on Earth!

Oh dear!

Sentences

Phrases

Message intended by the writer on page 8.

In three days' time the man will leave his family and go to the sea. He will stay there fishing for a month. He will then return to his family.

The verb "to be"

Some verbs are easier to spot than others.

It is easy to see that the words in the bubble can all be used as *doing* words.

But a verb is not always about *doing*. It can be a word about *being*.

London is the capital city of England.

Julius Caesar was a Roman general.

I am good at maths.

David is brilliant at running.

First of January, 2000, will be the first day of the twenty-first century.

Victoria used to be Queen of England.

The Vikings were very fierce warriors.

Our teacher is wonderful!

You were late this morning.

In each of these sentences, the verb is part of the verb *to be*. Which word (or group of words) is the verb (or verb-group) in each sentence?

The person who spots each part of the verb *to be* in each sentence should write it on the blackboard.

Can you think of any other parts of the verb *to be* which you can add to your list?

Go round the class and let each person make up a sentence using one part of the verb *to be*.

19

Sentences

Once upon a time, there was a witch. She was very fat and very greedy. Every day she ate twenty different meals. And the meals were all big. For instance, for breakfast, she gobbled down orange juice, cornflakes, bacon, eggs, sausages, baked beans, beef-burgers, toast, ice-cream and jelly. That was a small meal for her. For a mid-morning snack she ate soup, fish, meat, potatoes, carrots, peas, cabbage, baked beans, beef-burgers, spaghetti, an apple, an orange, ice-cream, jelly and bread and butter. Every day, of course, the witch grew fatter and fatter.

How many sentences are in this story?

How do we show the end of a sentence? How do we show that a new sentence is beginning?

Each sentence in the story has *one* verb (no verb-groups). Find the verb in each sentence.

In your language book:

Write the heading – *Verbs and Sentences*

A Copy and complete:

> A verb is a word of d_____ or b_____. Every
> sentence contains a v_____. If a group of words
> does not have a verb it is not a s_____. It is
> called a ph_____.
> One very common verb is the verb t__ b__.

B Look back at the story about the witch on page 20.
Copy and complete these sentences about it.
(The first sentence needs a *number* to complete it.)

> 1) There are _____ sentences in this story.
> 2) We show a new sentence is starting with a
>   _____.
> 3) We show the end of a sentence with a
>   _____.
> 4) Each sentence in the story has one verb. The
>   verbs in the story are _____, _____, _____,
>   _____, _____, _____, _____, _____.

C Copy out three of the sentences in the box on page
19. In each sentence underline the parts of the verb
to be.

D Copy out these sentences. Underline the verb in each one.

1) Most animals run away from their enemies.
2) An octopus sprays ink at its enemies.
3) A hedgehog rolls up in a ball.
4) A skunk makes a horrible smell.

E Write three sentences of your own about what you did last night. Underline all the verbs.

Adjectives: Making Sentences Grow

Here are some simple sentences:

The girl ate the apple.

The monster destroyed the city.

In the first sentence find two nouns (naming words).
Now find one verb (a word of doing or being).
Do the same for the second sentence.

We can make sentences grow by adding extra words.

The little girl ate the sour green apple.

The huge hairy monster destroyed the old city.

Which words have been added in the first sentence?
What sort of words are they?
What about the second sentence?

Nouns and *verbs* make up the main part of the
sentence each time. But *adjectives* make sentences
more interesting. They tell you more about the nouns.

An adjective describes a noun.

23

Look at these two sentences.

The tired old man sat on the hard wooden bench.

The ugly hook-nosed witch cast a terrible spell.

Find all the adjectives in those two sentences.
What would the sentences be without the adjectives?

Think of some good adjectives to add to these
sentences to make them more interesting.

The prince killed a dragon.

The man married the woman.

Word Identikit   *Work with a partner.*

big	hooded	ragged	blue	hooked
cheerful	long	drab	sharp	mean
short	smiling	grey	red	fat	pale
pimply	snub	greasy	pink	sparkling

The adjectives above will help you turn the sentences below into a description of a man, the way police build up identikit pictures of criminals. Without adjectives the sentences don't really tell you anything about the man – he could be anybody.

> The man had * eyes and a * nose.
> He had a * mouth.   He was wearing a * coat.

The * marks show where adjectives should be added. You can add two or three adjectives each time, but you must be careful to choose adjectives that go together well. (For instance, "smiling" goes well with "cheerful". But you couldn't put "mean" and "cheerful" together, because people aren't usually mean and cheerful at the same time.)

On a piece of scrap paper write out the sentences with adjectives wherever there is a *.

When you have finished, your teacher will ask some people to give their descriptions.

How many different men has the class described?

Remember that you were all using the same basic sentences. Adjectives are very important for helping people describe things clearly.

Think of some good adjectives to describe:

a witch.   a mouse.   your best friend.   25

In your language book:

Write the heading – *Making Sentences More Interesting*

A Copy and complete:

> Every sentence has a v_____. Some simple sentences are made up of just the v_____ and some n_____s. We can make the sentences more interesting by adding a_____s to describe the n_____s.

B Copy these sentences into your book. In each sentence, put a ring round the *verb*. Put boxes round each of the *nouns*. Underline all the *adjectives*.
The first one is done for you to show you how.

1) A <u>beautiful</u> | woman | (sang) a <u>short</u> <u>sad</u> | song |.
2) The little girl ate the sour green apple.
3) The huge hairy monster destroyed the old city.
4) The little dog ate the big juicy bone.
5) A young policeman chased the fat robber.
6) A white-faced, red-nosed clown threw a big yellow pie.

C Write out the sentences in question B, *without the adjectives*.

D Copy out these sentences and add some adjectives to make them more interesting.

> 1) The man ate the sandwich.
> 2) The cat climbed the tree.
> 3) A girl jumped out of the car.

E Use the adjectives from the *Word Identikit* on page 25 to write a description of a woman, in the same way that we wrote a description of a man.

> The woman had * eyes and a * nose. She had a * mouth. She was wearing a * dress and a * coat.

Parts of Speech: Pronouns

We know that words have different jobs to do in a sentence. One sort of word is a noun. What is a noun?

Another sort is a verb. What is a verb?

Another sort is an adjective. Can you remember what an adjective does?

Nouns, verbs and adjectives are called parts of speech. Different parts of speech do different jobs in a sentence.

Another part of speech is a *pronoun*.

"Pro" at the beginning of a word can mean "standing in place of". What do you think a pronoun stands in place of? Why do you think that?

---

(1) Tessa put the book into <u>Tessa's</u> bag.

(2) Simon ate <u>Simon's</u> dinner. Then <u>Simon</u> watched the T.V.

(3) The box was heavy, because <u>the box</u> had bricks in it.

In the sentences in the box some nouns are underlined. This is because we have used them in a funny way. We have used them where we would usually use a pronoun.

What words would we usually say instead of the underlined nouns in these sentences?

A pronoun stands in place of a noun.

28

In the next box of sentences, the pronouns are underlined. Which nouns do they stand for?
    Work out what the sentences would be if we had used the nouns instead of pronouns.

---

(1) The dog ran to _its_ master.

(2) The headteacher overslept, so _he_ was late for school.

(3) Mary had a little lamb;
    She ate _it_ with mint sauce.
    So everywhere that Mary went
    The lamb went too, of course.

There are lots of pronouns.

Here are 31 of the most common ones. These pronouns can be split into three groups.

> I   your   them   she   yourselves   us
> myself   ourselves   yours   he   its   itself
> mine   my   his   themselves   you
> yourself   himself   we   him   hers   herself
> our   theirs   they   it   their
> ours   her   me

The first group are pronouns to do with I or we .

1 That's when I'm talking about myself, or me and my friends.

2 That's when I'm talking about you — one or more of you.

The second group are pronouns to do with you .

The third group are to do with he, she, it or they .

3 That's when I'm talking about someone or something else.

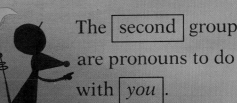

Place the pronoun

Your teacher will draw three columns on the board, headed:

First person pronouns	Second person pronouns	Third person pronouns
I we	you	he she it they

Look back to the list of 31 pronouns. If you know in which column a pronoun fits, put your hand up. Your teacher will choose people to write on the board in what they think are the correct columns. As each pronoun is written up, everyone else should put thumbs up if they think the pronoun is in the correct place, or thumbs down if they think it's in the wrong place.

Your teacher will tell you whether you've chosen correctly or not.

Which pronouns fit into the spaces in this story?

Once upon a time, there was a little ghost called Sidney. __ lived in an old castle and ___ best friend was a rat called Alice. One day, Sidney and Alice were playing in the dungeons, when ____ found a piece of paper with writing and pictures on __. Sidney handed __ to Alice.

"_ can't read," __ said. "___'d better read __."

"O.K." said Alice. ___ stared hard at the piece of paper. ___ eyes grew wider and wider. "Gosh," ___ said at last. "This is a treasure map. __ says there's buried treasure hidden in the castle."

"Golly," said Sidney. "Can __ go and hunt for __?"

Now let someone try and read the story without using pronouns – try to put the right noun in every space, like this:

> "Once upon a time, there was a little ghost called Sidney. *Sidney* lived in an old castle and *Sidney*'s best friend was a rat called Alice..."

It makes the story sound very silly!

Ban the pronoun!

Work with a partner. Choose a story or a short passage from a reading book. With your partner work out which words in the story are pronouns, and which nouns they are standing in place of. Underline them faintly in pencil. Practise reading the story, saying the nouns instead of the pronouns each time.

When you have had time to practise, your teacher will ask some pairs to read their stories aloud.

Thank goodness for pronouns!

In your language book:

Write the heading – *Parts of Speech: Pronouns*

A Copy and complete:

> Nouns, verbs and adjectives are called
> p____s of s____. These different sorts of
> words do different jobs in a sentence. Another
> p____ of s____ is the pronoun. A p____
> stands in place of a n____.

B Draw three columns like the ones your teacher
drew on the board. Put all the pronouns from the
list on page 29 into the correct columns in your
book.

First *person* *pronouns*	*Second* *person* *pronouns*	*Third* *person* *pronouns*

C Copy these sentences. Fill the spaces with the
correct pronouns. All the pronouns are from page
29.

> 1) The king wore _____ crown.
> 2) The children came into school. Then _____ sat
>   down.
> 3) Pick up your pen and put _____ in the pencil
>   case.
> 4) Beth feeds _____ goldfish every day.
> 5) We write _____ names inside _____ wellies so
>   they won't get mixed up.

D Copy these passages, but wherever a word or group of words is in *italics*, replace it with the correct pronoun.

   1) The boy ran as fast as *the boy* could. *The boy* was trying to win the race. *The race* was an important one, and *the boy* had been training hard for *the race*.

   2) Steve and Sally went to the shops. *Steve and Sally* bought some sweets. Steve ate all *Steve's* sweets, but Sally saved *Sally's* till *Steve and Sally* got home. Then *Sally* ate *the sweets*.

   3) My brother and I are going to visit our gran. *My brother and I* like going to see *our gran*. *Our gran* gives *my brother and me* cakes for tea.

E Choose a passage from your reading book with at least five pronouns in it. Copy out the passage, but instead of the pronouns write the *nouns* that they stand for. Underline these nouns.

Sentences and Subjects

Every sentence has a verb.

Find the verbs in these sentences:

The old man sang a very long song.
Elizabeth kicked the football.
The Houses of Parliament stand beside the River
　　Thames.
Every night, Margaret eats two plates of chips for
　　her tea.
Elephants live in Africa and India.
She told us a story.
Unfortunately, the treasure map crumbled to dust.
It was very old.

Every verb has a subject.

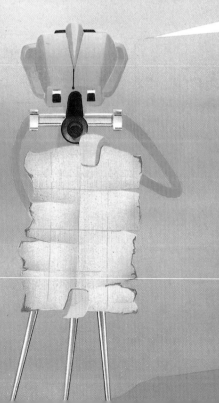

The subjects of the verbs
in these sentences are:

The old man
Elizabeth
The Houses of Parliament
Margaret
Elephants
She
the treasure map
It

What would you say a *subject* is?
Can you work out any rules about:

> where in the sentence you might find it?
> where you might find it in relation to the verb?
> what sort of part of speech it might be?

Study the examples and have a think. Now work out what the subjects and verbs are in the sentences at the foot of the page:

1) Ask your teacher to write each sentence up on the board like this:

S   V

Cinderella sat

among the ashes.

2) The person who spots the verb underlines it and marks it with a V. (Look at the example above.)
3) The person who spots the subject puts a wiggly line under it and marks it with an S. (Look at the example above.)

> Cinderella sat among the ashes.
> Luckily, her fairy godmother found her there.
> She waved her magic wand.
> I like baked beans on toast.
> My dad likes baked beans on toast too.

35

In each example below the *subjects* of the sentences have been torn off the paper. What do you think they might have been?

is a really good T.V. programme.

is Prime Minister of Great Britain.

swims the fastest in our class.

has beautiful handwriting.

is the best pop singer in the world.

can run faster than any other animal.

In the next set of examples the subjects have been left, but the *verb and the rest of the sentence* have been torn away.

What do you think they should be in each case?

The pirate captain

It

The Queen of Britain

Our teacher

Dracula

We

Mount Everest

Some very simple sentences are just made up of a *subject* and a *verb*, like this: –

The ghost disappeared. Snoopy barks.

The Queen waved. Flowers grow.

In fact, all sentences, no matter how long, are based on those two things – *subject* and *verb*. Look: –

> **S V**
>
> With a slight smile, the boy jumped lightly out of the window.

> **S V**
>
> The boy jumped.

Look back to the first list of sentences we gave, on page 34. For each of those sentences, work out what the basic *subject + verb* is.

Your teacher can write them on the board, and some people can do the underlining (wiggly for a subject, straight for a verb,) and labelling (**S** and **V**).

There are lots of games you can play by mixing up the subjects of sentences. Look back to the subjects on page 36. Try pairing them up with the bits of sentences above them – those *without* subjects. You can make some very silly sentences!

Dracula has beautiful handwriting.

Dip into the future

This game matches up subjects with sentence-endings, and pretends to tell your fortune. You need two boxes, one marked *subject* and one marked *verb+rest of sentence*.

Every player needs two small pieces of paper. On the first piece you write your own name. This piece should then be folded up and put in the box marked *subject*.

On the second piece of paper, you write a "prediction" (without a subject), like the ones below. You can choose one of these or make up another of the same sort.

Whatever you choose to write, it should start with a verb, like the examples we have given.

The predictions should then be folded up and put into the box marked *verb+rest of sentence*.

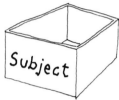

Subject

should not eat any more chocolate this week.

will have seventeen children.

will find a five pound note.

will become Prime Minister.

will marry a very rich person and live in a castle.

will appear on T.U. within three years.

will live to be 106.

will run for Britain in the Olympic Games.

Verb and rest of sentence

Finally the teacher chooses some people to pick out one piece of paper from each box. First, pick the subject, then the rest of the sentence. The two together will make a prediction for a member of the class.

Good Luck!

In your language book:

Write the heading – *Sentences and Subjects*

A Copy and complete:

> Every sentence has a s_____. The s_____ goes with the v_____ and is usually found just in front of the v_____.
>
> Some very simple sentences are made up of just a s_____ and a v_____.

B Copy these sentences. For each one, underline and label the subjects and verbs. The first one is done for you, to show you how.

>   **S**   **V**
> 1) The plane flew over the city.
> 2) Rabbits eat grass and other plants.
> 3) The guard checks the tickets on a train.
> 4) Penguins live near the South Pole.
> 5) Babies cry.
> 6) We come to school on weekdays.
> 7) At weekends, we stay at home.

C Copy out these subjects and finish each one off with a suitable verb and rest of sentence. Underline and label your verbs.

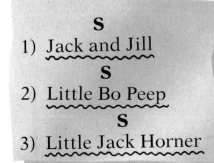

>   **S**
> 1) Jack and Jill
>   **S**
> 2) Little Bo Peep
>   **S**
> 3) Little Jack Horner

>   **S**
> 4) My best friend
>   **S**
> 5) I

D Copy out these sentences, putting a suitable subject into each blank space. Underline and label your subjects.

             S   **V**

1) ~~~~~ <u>had</u> a little lamb.

             S   **V**

2) ~~~~~ <u>jumped</u> over the moon.

             S   **V**

3) ~~~~~ <u>ran</u> up the clock.

             S   **V**

4) ~~~~~ <u>is</u> the fastest runner in our class.

             S   **V**

5) ~~~~~ <u>is</u> my favourite colour.

E Here are some very simple S+V sentences. Make each one into a longer sentence by adding something more. You can add extra words at the beginning or at the end. The first one is done to show you how.

1) The dog barked.
   Last night, the dog barked at my brother.

2) I sang.
3) The girl ran.
4) The moon rose.
5) Ducks swim.

Punctuation: Making Sense with Sentences

```
hello everybody it's nice
to meet you my name is
Frankie as you can see I
am a computer my master
programs me to do all sorts
of things he has programmed
me to tell jokes jokes are
good fun
```

Frankie is a computer. If he could talk he would have a robot voice, like a Dalek. It would not change tone, and he would never pause for breath. Can you read his message aloud in a robot voice, without stopping for breath at all?

```
there is something wrong
with the way I write things
people don't understand my
jokes there's no point in
telling jokes if nobody
understands them please
teach me how to write like
a person
```

What's the difference between the way people talk and the way Frankie talks? What's the difference between the way people write and the way Frankie writes? What would you tell him to do so that he'd write like a person?

41

Frankie's programmer tried to program him to put full stops and capital letters in his writing. This is what happened. Try to read it out loud.

```
Hello everybody it's nice.
  To meet you my name.  Is
Frankie as you can.  See I
am a computer my master.
Programs me to do all.  Sorts
of things he has programmed
me to tell jokes jokes.  Are
         good fun.
```

What went wrong? Can you think of a way the programmer could explain so that Frankie gets it right?

Where should the full stops and capital letters go in

Frankie's first two messages?

Here are some of Frankie's jokes.

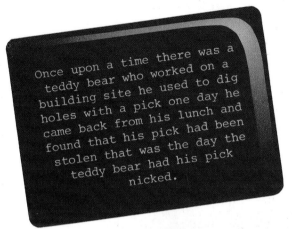

Once upon a time there was a teddy bear who worked on a building site he used to dig holes with a pick one day he came back from his lunch and found that his pick had been stolen that was the day the teddy bear had his pick nicked.

once there was a man who slept with his head under a pillow one day this man woke up without any teeth the fairies had taken them away.

a man went to the doctor because he thought he was a pair of curtains the doctor told him to pull himself together another man went to the doctor because he thought he was a pack of cards the doctor said he'd deal with him later.

When we are talking, we break up our speech into groups of words that make sense, to help our listeners understand what we are saying. We use short pauses and changes of voice to do this.

When we are writing, we can show these pauses and changes by putting a full stop at the end of a sentence, and a capital letter to show that a new sentence is beginning.

One member of the class should read each joke out very slowly, pausing at the ends of sentences, so that it makes sense.

The rest of the class can call out *"Full Stop – Capital Letter"* whenever one sentence ends and another begins.

The rules of language are very complicated. Nobody has yet been able to program a computer to use full stops and capital letters correctly all the time. It is something that human beings can do, but computers can't. Human beings can work out where the breaks in sentences come, even though they don't always know why.

Let's think why. Here is one of Frankie's jokes with the full stops to show sentences.

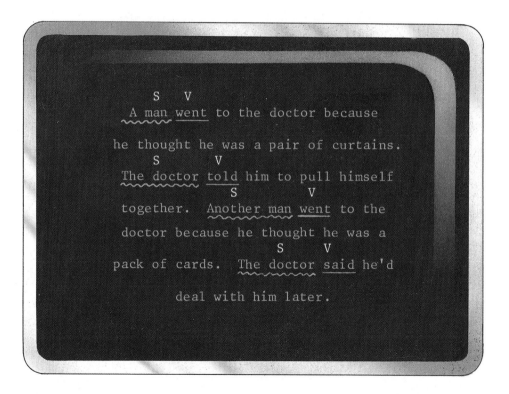

Very often – *not always*, but very often – a new *subject and verb* can mean the beginning of a new sentence.

This is because a new *subject and verb* often means the beginning of a new idea in what we are saying. **When we start a fresh thought, we usually start a fresh sentence**.

In your language book:

Write the heading – *Sense and Sentences*

A Copy and complete:

> A s_____ is a group of words that make s_____ on their own. Every s_____ has a s_____ and a v_____. We break up our writing into s_____s to help our readers understand what we mean. We use p_____ marks to show where sentences begin and end. A f_____ s_____ shows the end of a s_____. A c_____ l_____ shows that a new s_____ is beginning.

B Copy out the first two of Frankie's jokes and put capital letters and full stops in them to show where each sentence begins and ends.

C Read the jokes you have written out loud (under your breath), pausing where you have put full stops. Have you punctuated the jokes correctly?

D Copy out this passage and split it up into sentences so that it makes sense.

> Here is the news this afternoon a train carrying jelly crashed with a train carrying fresh cream police say that rail services will be running a trifle late on the M1 a lorry has spilt a load of hair restorer police are combing the area finally we have news of the man who stole a calendar he got twelve months.

 Punctuation: Using Punctuation Marks

In the last chapter, we said that people use their voices to break up their speech. They break up their speech into groups of words that make sense. How do they do this? How do we show it in writing?

You use your voice in many other ways to help your listener. You can use it to show you are asking a question.

How does someone's voice show that he's asking a question?

You can use your voice to show you are making a statement of fact, like the *answer* to a question. How is this different from a questioning voice?

These differences are known as *tones of voice*. You can raise the tone of your voice to show that you are angry, or to give a warning. You can change your tone to show that you are making a joke.

Let some people try reading the words in these speech bubbles in the right tones of voice.

Which pictures show ⓐ statements ⓑ questions ⓒ a raised voice ⓓ a joke?

Faces are important too. The *expressions* on people's faces change as they talk, depending on what they are saying. Change your face to make these expressions.

surprised   angry   frightened   questioning   joking   serious

In writing, we cannot use pauses, tone of voice or expressions on the face to show how we want to say something. Instead, we use *punctuation marks*.

Here are some punctuation marks you should know.

What is each one called?

Which of these punctuation marks do we use to show the following?

The end of a phrase or sentence where someone is raising the tone of his voice.

The end of an ordinary phrase or sentence.

The end of a question.

The end of a phrase or sentence that is not to be taken seriously.

Gobble-de-gook

Even nonsense language can make *some* sense.

Work with a partner. Read out the gobble-de-gook conversations in the picture story above, using the punctuation marks to work out the right tones of voice and facial expressions.

Then try to work out what the story is about.

If you have time, you can make up some more gobble-de-gook conversation, to make a short play of your own.

Your teacher can choose a few pairs to act out their gobble-de-gook conversations to the class.

Can the rest of the class work out what is going on?

Punctuation marks break up what we write, into sentences that make sense. They also show *how* we should say the sentences.

The Comma

There is another common punctuation mark that you will have seen in books.

In fact, there is one of them in this sentence.

What does it look like?

It is called the *comma*. Commas show very short breaks *within sentences*. They help the reader understand what the sentence means.

Look at these examples, and listen to your teacher read them out:

Can you see how the comma changes the sense of the sentence very slightly? What difference does it make?

At the moment, don't try to use commas much in your own writing. Just make sure you get the full stops right. But keep an eye out for the way commas are used in the books you read. Let the commas help you make sense of what the author is saying. This will also help you get an idea of the best ways to use commas.

50

There is one *special* use of the comma which is easy to learn. Look back to the story about The Greedy Witch, on page 20. There are lots of commas in that story. What special job are the commas doing in the lists of the witch's food?

How are these two sentences different?

The monster liked to eat silver paper, gold candlesticks, leather boots and old socks.

The monster liked to eat silver, paper, gold, candlesticks, leather, boots and old socks.

Where should there be commas in these sentences?

1) I like playing football cricket tennis and rounders.
2) The spoilt little boy cried screamed kicked and spat.
3) The witch had a long thin knobbly nose.
4) On holiday we sat on the beach swam in the sea went on the pier and spent a day at the fairground.

If the last item in a list begins with "and", do you need a comma before the "and"?

Commas are used to separate the items in a list.

In your language book:

Write the heading – *Punctuation Marks and the Comma*

A Copy and complete:

> P_____ m_____s break up what we write into s_____s that make s_____. A qu_____ m_____ shows that a sentence should be read in a questioning voice. An ex_____ m_____ shows that a sentence should be read in a raised voice. It can also show that someone is joking.

B Copy out these sentences and punctuate them – use capital letters, full stops, question marks and exclamation marks.

> 1) where is my dinner
> 2) don't do that
> 3) cotton comes from a plant grown in warm countries
> 4) it is very cold at the north pole
> 5) how far is it to your house
> 6) help – I'm stuck in a tree

C Copy and complete:

> A c_____ is another p_____ m_____. It looks like a f_____ s_____ with a little tail. It is used to separate the items in a l_____. It can also show short breaks inside s_____s.

D Copy out sentences 1–4 on page 51, and put commas in the correct places.

E Copy out these sentences and put commas in the correct places.

> 1) Cakes are made with flour eggs butter and milk.
> 2) At the zoo they had huge grey elephants sweet little lion cubs two-humped camels and a giraffe.
> 3) The four longest rivers in the world are the Nile the Amazon the Yangtze-Kiang and the Lena.
> 4) At school we write stories draw pictures read books and work out maths problems.

F Copy out these little plays and put in all the punctuation as necessary.

> 1) *Dentist*: have your teeth ever been checked
>   *Patient*: no they've always been white
>
> 2) *Doctor*: how did your feet get so badly scalded
>   *Patient*: I was making soup for my tea
>   *Doctor*: did you spill it
>   *Patient*: no I just followed the instructions on the tin
>   *Doctor*: what did it say on the tin
>   *Patient*: stand in hot water for ten minutes

 # Punctuation: The Apostrophe

What are these punctuation marks called?

What is each used for in writing?
How do we show the same things when we are speaking?

There is one punctuation mark which is *not* used to show pauses, breaks between groups of words, or tones of voice. It is called the *apostrophe*. It looks like a flying comma.

The apostrophe is found *inside words*. It has two uses – it can show:

1) ownership
2) that a word has been *shortened* – usually by pushing two words together to make one.

At the moment, we need only look at the second use:

The Apostrophe in shortened words

I'm	mustn't	you're	it'll
we've	don't	he's	can't

All of the words in the box are made up of two words pushed together.

What are the two words in each case? (If you're not sure, try putting the word into a sentence – that should help you find the *meaning*.)

When you have worked out the answers, some people can write them on the board like this:

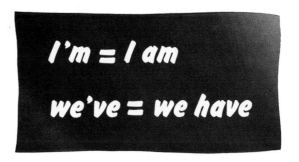

I'm = I am

we've = we have

With a different coloured chalk, some people can put a ring round the letters which are missed out in each case. Like this:

I'm = I(a)m

we've = we (ha)ve

Look hard at all the examples on the board and try to find an answer to this question:

> When two words are shortened into one word, *where* do we put the apostrophe?

What would the shortened forms of these words be?

should not   I would   we are   were not
    she will   you have   of the clock

Again, if you're not sure, imagine the words in a short sentence.

When you've worked them out, write them up on the board, like this:

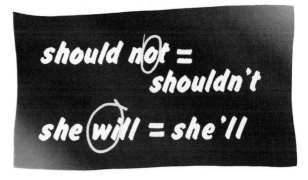

should n(o)t = shouldn't

she (wil)l = she'll

Shortened forms are more common in speech than in writing. Why?

Sometimes in poetry, poets use apostrophes to shorten words so that they will fit into a line. In each of these examples, what does the short form stand for? And what letters have been missed out?

There ne'er were such thousands of leaves on a tree,
Nor of people in church or in park,
As the thousands of stars that looked down upon me,
And that glittered and winked in the dark.

'Twas the night before Christmas
And all through the house,
Not a creature was stirring,
Not even a mouse.

I wandered lonely as a cloud
That floats on high o'er vales and hills...

In your language book:

Write the heading – *The Apostrophe in Shortened Words*

A Copy and complete:

> The apostrophe is a p_____ m_____ which is found inside w_____s. It can show that l_____s have been missed out of a word. This often happens when two words are pushed together. The a_____ goes where the letter or letters are m_____.

B Write these words out in full. Show which letters are missed out in the short form by putting a ring around them. The first one is done to show you how.

I'll	=	I (sha)ll	haven't	=
you've	=		it'd	=
she's	=		could've	=
it's	=		we're	=
wouldn't	=		wasn't	=
isn't	=		they're	=
mustn't	=		they've	=
I'm	=		o'clock	=

C Copy out these sentences, changing the words in italics to short forms. Make sure you put the apostrophes in the right places.

1) *I would* like to come but I *cannot*.
2) *They have* just got back from their holidays.
3) *It is* raining today. *It will* probably rain tomorrow too.
4) You *must not* do that – *it is* dangerous!
5) People who live in glass houses *should not* throw stones.

57

D In these sentences the apostrophes have been left out. Copy the sentences, putting apostrophes in where necessary.

> 1) Its too cold to play outside.
> 2) Were looking forward to the party.
> 3) Dont stop writing till youve finished the page.
> 4) Ive read all these books, havent I?
> 5) Your mother says youll have to pay for the broken window.

There should be *seven* apostrophes in these sentences altogether. Have you got the right number?

E In this short play punctuation has been missed out – apostrophes, full stops, capital letters, question marks, exclamation marks and commas. Copy it out and put all the punctuation in correctly.

> *emma:* whats got a lot of legs pink eyes yellow wings and a striped black body
> *tim:* I dont know what is it
> *emma:* I dont know either but its crawling up the back of your neck

Spoken Language versus Written Language

Spoken and written language have a lot in common. They both use *words*. And they are both concerned with getting *meaning* across between one person and another.

But in many other ways they are very different. For instance, you use different parts of your body for speaking and writing.

What parts of the body are used in spoken language?

What parts of the body are used in written language?

And there is the question of equipment. Do you need any extra equipment (apart from your own body) to speak? To write?

Take votes in your class on these questions:

Which is easier, speaking or writing?
Which is quicker, speaking or writing?
Which lasts longer – spoken or written language?
Which helps you remember best – spoken or
    written language?
Which is easier to check – spoken or written
    language?

Spoken language is useful in many ways, but it can sometimes let you down. For instance, there is the famous story of the general in the First World War who sent this message back to headquarters:

> "The Germans are advancing on the west flank. Please send reinforcements."

What does that message mean?
    Unfortunately, the message had to be passed on from one messenger to another, and mistakes were made. By the time it reached headquarters, it sounded like this:

> "The Germans are dancing on a wet plank. Please send three and fourpence."

(There is a funny story called "Send Three and Fourpence, We're Going to Dance", which is based on the same sort of mistake. It is by Jan Mark and is in the Puffin book *Nothing To Be Afraid Of*. Perhaps if you have it in your school library, your teacher will read it to you sometime.)

Chinese Whispers

The old party game, Chinese Whispers, is based on the way messages can be changed as they are passed on. Try it for yourselves and see what happens with your messages.

Someone thinks of a message – not too short and not too long. It's a good idea to write it down and give it to the teacher. Then this person whispers the message softly and quickly into his/her neighbour's ear. This neighbour then whispers what he/she has heard to the neighbour on the other side, and so on, until the message has been passed right round the class or group.

The whisperer cannot repeat the message, and each listener must make the best sense of it possible, before passing it on – so make sure you whisper actual words (no matter how daft they may seem), not just gibberish.

When the message has reached the end of its journey, the last listener can say what he/she has heard. And the person who gave the message in the first place can say what it started as.

See how much the message has got changed on its travels.

KIM'S GAME

Kim's Game is another party game which shows how spoken language can let you down. The game leader (your teacher?) produces a tray of about 15 different objects, which you are allowed to look at for about three minutes.

The tray is then hidden, and for another few minutes you have to keep occupied doing other things. (You could have another go at Chinese Whispers!) People are then chosen to try listing the objects on the tray, scoring one point for each one they remember.

Try playing this game with half the group "cheating" – that is, using a pencil and paper to note the objects when they see them first. The other half will probably find that using the memory can be harder than using a pencil.

Can you think of some other occasions when we need *written* rather than *spoken* language?

Why was it written down?

During every day you probably make use of written language on many, many occasions. Often you don't even notice it.

Try now to make a list on scrap paper of every single bit of reading that you did *yesterday* – not just books and so on, but things like street signs, T.V. subtitles, and even the writing on the cornflakes box at breakfast time!

Go through the day bit by bit and remember what you did, particularly the reading at each stage:

> First thing in the morning;
> The later part of the morning;
> Around lunch time;
> In the afternoon;
> Around tea-time;
> In the evening.

How long a list can you make?

Now, why was each of those things written down? Tell your teacher of any good reasons you can think of.

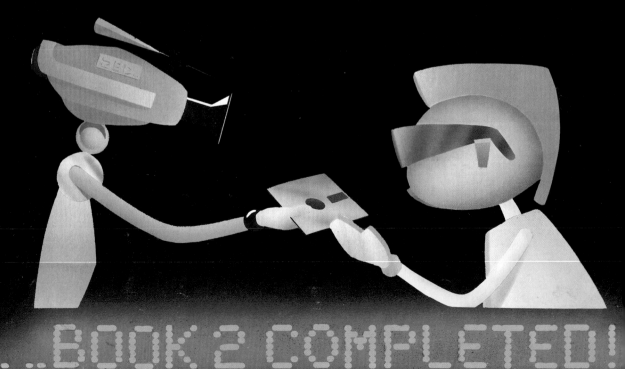

.. ..BOOK 2 COMPLETED!